Understanding Nature Vol. 2
Fun Outdoor Activities for Kids

By Rick McKeon

Preface

This is the second volume in the *Understanding Nature* series. This one is just for kids! Well, it's really for adults who love kids and want them to experience wonder and excitement about the natural world.

If you are an adult who works with kids, consider this a resource book of fun activities to help spark their interest in nature. Take this book along when you go out for a hike or just on a picnic. These activities can be used out in the forest, at the local park, or in your own backyard!

My purpose for writing this volume is to encourage young people to get outdoors and enjoy the natural world. The benefits are many - exercise and fresh air, sparking curiosity and stimulating the imagination, developing a healthy attitude toward nature and other people, and just plain having FUN! Kids need to get out and be kids in a healthy environment.

One Caution: Don't make work out of it - keep it fun! Instead of an academic study with things to memorize and quizzes to take, encourage your kids to enjoy learning about nature as an enjoyable hobby. After all, this is the way Richard Feynman learned from his dad. He turned out OK.

So, let's go out and have some fun discovering the natural world!

I would love to hear your comments and suggestions. Send me an email at rmckeon5@gmail.com

Let's get started!
Rick

Table of Contents

1. Count the Numbers   4
    Activity 1.1 Find Examples of One through Eight
2. Strange Creatures in the Forest   9
    Activity 2.1 Strange Creatures and Their Stories
3. Many Colors   13
    Activity 3.1 The Colors of Nature
4. Who Lives Here?   17
    Activity 4.1 A Variety of Homes
5. I Know You Even With My Eyes Closed!   20
    Activity 5.1 I Know You by Touch
    Activity 5.2 I Know You by Smell
6. Nature Close Up   24
    Activity 6.1 What Did You Notice?
7. New Growth   26
    Activity 7.1 What Characterizes New Growth?
8. Vines   28
    Activity 8.1 Now I know How Vines Behave
9. Mushrooms   31
    Activity 9.1 Beautiful or Yucky?
10. What Happened Here?   34
    Activity 10.1 You Are Sherlock Holmes
11. Persistence   37
    Activity 11.1 Find Examples of Nature's Persistence
12. Nature's Geometry   41
    Activity 12.1 How Many Can You Find?
13. Treasure Hunting   44
    Activity 13.1 Find a Treasure to Take Home
14. Nature Sings   45
    Activity 14.1 Hearing Nature's Sounds
    Activity 14.2 Imitating Natural Sounds
Meet the Author   47
Other Books By Rick McKeon   48

1. Count the Numbers

Here's a fun activity that will get your kids looking closely at what lies all around them. It's an easy one that everyone can enjoy. Try to find examples of all of the numbers from one to eight. Don't be too strict on the interpretation. Just have fun with it. I bet you will be surprised at what they come up with! Here are a few pictures to get you thinking.

One Leaf Left on the Branch

A Tree Splits in Two

A Rock Splits into Three Parts

Four Parts to a Seed Pod

Five Lobes to Each Leaf

Six New Prickly Pear Fruit

Seven Leaves on a Stem

Eight Leaves per Cluster

Activity 1.1 Find Examples of One through Eight

Set a time limit and send them out to see how many examples of the numbers one through eight they can find. It will be fun for everyone to show what he or she has found and explain why it is an example of that number. Maybe not everyone will agree on each example, but I bet you will have a lot of fun in the process!

2. Strange Creatures in the Forest

Here is a fun game to stimulate the imagination. Pretend there are strange creatures in the forest. Some are friendly, some are funny, and some may be scary. Search around to find these creatures in the trees, the rocks, and even in the clouds. If you have to add some rocks for eyes or move some things around, that's OK - just have fun with it. Have the kids make up a story about each creature - what its name is, how long it has been in the forest, what it likes to do, etc. I bet you will hear some whoppers!

Here are some of my favorites to spark your imagination.

A Tree Walking down the Valley

Horace the Horse

Fred the Fungus

The Running Girl

Activity 2.1 Strange Creatures and Their Stories

Use you imagination to see strange creatures and interesting scenes in the rocks, trees, water and clouds all around you. Is there a rock that looks like it might come to life? Is there a bump on a tree that looks like a face? Maybe it's a creature trying to get out! Once you find these creatures or scenes in the clouds, make up a story about them. Where did they come from? What language do they speak? Do they have a family?

As in the last activity, let go of strict rules and let your imagination loose. Kids should experience excitement and wonder, experience strange new worlds, and learn about their creative side before the world and adult responsibilities take over. There's plenty of time for them to get serious and worry about paying the bills a few years from now.

3. Many Colors

Out in the natural world there are a multitude of colors. Often we enjoy our time in the wild but don't focus specifically on the many colors all around us. Here are a few photos to get you thinking.

15

Activity 3.1 The Colors of Nature

In this activity we are going to discover the amazing variety of colors in nature. I bet you will discover colors and shades of color that you never paid attention to before!

Pick a category like plants, animals, or rocks and see how many different colors you can discover. Just one tree will display many different colors - not just brown for the trunk and green for the leaves, but many different colors just in the trunk!

4. Whose Lives Here?

Out in the woods you will discover a wonderful variety of animals. Each one seems to prefer a different type of home. The pile of twigs shown in the photo above belongs to a packrat. Carpenter ants created the pile of sawdust shown in the next photo. In the last picture a lizard went scurrying out of this hole just before I took the shot.

Activity 4.1 A Variety of Homes

See how many different types of homes you can find and ask yourself why each animal prefers this type of home to others. Birds spend a lot of time in the trees and usually prefer their homes up there. But some birds spend a lot of time on the ground. Guess where their homes are!

5. I Know You Even With My Eyes Closed!

We rely greatly on our vision to understand the natural world, but we are also very perceptive using just the sense of touch or the sense of smell. Young people are often amazed to find out how perceptive they can be using these senses!

The aspen bark shown above is smooth and silky but the ponderosa pine bark shown below is rough and flaky. The two flowers shown below have very different scents. Rocks can be rough or smooth. A pine needle has a much different shape from an oak leaf. So, you can see there are all kinds of possibilities to identify things with your eyes closed.

With both of the activities below start with something pretty obvious and then make it a little more subtle. For example, two rocks might both be pretty smooth but maybe one is a little smoother than the other, or maybe it has a slightly different shape or size.

Activity 5.1 I Know You by Touch

Show two different rocks. Then, while blindfolded, hand them one of the rocks. Can they identify which one it is just by touching it? Then have them explain how they knew which one it was - texture of the surface, sharp edges, etc.

The same activity can be done with a couple of sticks or leaves. Just use whatever is handy. Here we are again immersing young people in the beauty and wonder of the natural world!

Activity 5.2 I Know You by Smell

This one might be a little more tricky because we don't usually know the smell of wildflowers, but maybe we can learn something along the way. Show two different wildflowers and see if they can identify them only through the sense of smell. If someone gets it right the first time, see if he or she can give a reason for the correct identification. This could lead to some interesting discussion.

You might want to expand on this activity. Did you know that ponderosa pine bark smells like vanilla? Crush a walnut tree leaf and smell it. Can you smell the walnuts?

6. Nature Close Up

On your next trip take a magnifying glass or hand-held microscope along. I'm always amazed at the details I find. They were there all along, but I just never noticed them before having a closer look!

For an interesting collection of photomicrographs see my book called "Nature's Small World." I set that one up so you have to guess first and then go to the back of the book to find out what the object is.

Here's a picture of the underside of a leaf taken through a hand-held microscope. It looks like a picture of suburban streets taken from an airplane. If you think about it, there are reasons for the similarities. Pretty amazing!

Activity 6.1 What Did You Notice?

Pass the magnifying glass around and let the kids experiment looking as closely as possible at different objects. What details did they notice about those objects that they didn't know were there before? See who can find the most unusual things. Who knows where this conversation might lead! It could lead to questions they take back to their science teacher.

7. New Growth

In the spring you will see new growth everywhere! It's exciting to see new shoots peaking up through the snow or tender new leaves on desert plants. We can always recognize new growth. But how do we distinguish new growth from the established plant?

Here are some things to consider:

1. Color: Is the new growth a different color from the established plant?
2. Size: New growth is usually smaller.
3. Position: Is it at the tip of the branches? It might not be.
4. Texture: Is the new growth softer, more pliable or more tender? Many times things that are going to become sharp thorns start out soft and pliable. It's only when they dry out and harden that they become painful and dangerous stickers.

Activity 7.1 Look for New Growth

This activity works best in the spring of the year. You might be out in the forest or looking at cracks in the sidewalk. In the spring there is new growth everywhere!

Look for signs of new growth. Once you find it, start to question what distinguishes new growth from the established plant. See how many factors characterize the new growth you are seeing.

Kids can be so perceptive! I bet you will be surprised at what they come up with.

8. Vines

Vines are amazing plants! They search for something to climb on, and will change direction depending on what they find they can get a hold of.

The pictures below show how vines have grabbed on to another plant for stability.

Activity 8.1 How Do Vines Behave?

Look closely at a vine to see if you can determine how it behaves. Look for attachment points. Once it found something to hold on to did it change direction? Can you predict where it will go next? Come back in a week or so to see if you were right.

9. Mushrooms

Mushrooms are amazing! Some are delicious and some are deadly. As far as appearance goes, they range from beautiful to downright scary. The lifecycle of a mushroom can be very complex, but for now we just want to see how many different kinds we can find.

Activity 9.1 Beautiful or Yucky?

If it has been a wet year you may find hundreds of mushroom on a single hike. As you are hiking see how many different kinds you can notice. If you find an unusual one take a picture and, when you get home see if you can determine what kind it is. The study of mushrooms can last a lifetime!

10. What Happened Here?

As you are hiking along be on the lookout for interesting places that tell a story. Once you find that special place, spend some time playing "nature detective." Look at the scene and see if you can determine what has happened in the past to make it look the way it does today. Can you determine what might happen in the future and how long it will take? Maybe there are several possible alternate futures to consider.

In the picture above what has happened? It appears that a tree has fallen across a small wash and dirt is collecting above it creating a level spot. Is it causing water to collect there so that the plants in the wash above it can flourish? Could it ever rain hard enough for the whole thing to wash away?

Here are a few more examples to get the creative juices flowing.

Activity 10.1 You Are Sherlock Holmes

Once you find that special place, set up the scene and give a few clues. Then let the kids play detective and come up with theories about what has happened and why. Many changes take a long time and maybe there is a process that is going on right now. Have them speculate about how long ago this event happened and what the future may hold. Make a game out of it and speculate about alternate futures.

If it's the spring of the year, see if they can determine why the snow is melting more quickly in some spots than others. If it has rained recently, can they tell if certain tracks were made before or after the rain?

11. Persistence

Nature can exhibit amazing persistence and tenacity. Plants and animals can exist and even thrive under very difficult circumstances. When I first saw the old Alligator Juniper shown above I thought for sure it was dead, but then I walked around to the other side and noticed some green needles. I wondered, "How can there be green needles on this dead tree?" Then I noticed a thin strip of bark. It was just enough to supply nutrients to those green leaves!

Here are some other examples of life flourishing in unexpected places. It amazes me how plants can grow out of a tiny crack in a rock!

Activity 11.1 Find Examples of Nature's Persistence

Look for examples of life taking hold in difficult circumstances. It might be a tree growing out of a crack in a rock or a plant all by itself in a desert that gets almost no rain. Up in the high mountains you will find ancient trees that have survived hundreds of severe winters or delicate grasses that flourish each spring.

Find a place where there has been a forest fire and see how quickly life comes back. Which plants come back first? It would be interesting to visit the same place a year later and look for changes.

12. Nature's Geometry

If you look closely you will see many geometric forms in nature - circles, triangles, cones, and many others. You will find these forms in plants, animals and insects, rock crystals, dried mud flats, things that animals build, etc.

The anthill shown above has a conical shape. I have watched ants at work bringing up grains of sand to build their home below the ground. They carry the sand to the rim of the cone and drop it over the edge. They don't drop it before getting to the rim because it would roll back down, and of course, they don't carry it all the way down the other side because they don't have to. If they continue doing this randomly in all directions a cone results.

You will find the old miners did the same thing and a lot of their test holes have a conical form. That makes sense because they were conserving energy like the ants do. But the strange thing is that volcanic craters and impact craters on the moon take the same form. Is conservation of energy involved there too? OK, so maybe I'm getting too philosophical for your kids. Lets just look for geometric forms in nature.

Activity 12.1 How Many Can You Find?

Stop for a little break and look around to see how many different geometric forms you can spot. You'll be surprised how many interesting things a group of kids can discover! There are leaves that look like triangles or hearts. Quartz crystals have a hexagonal shape. A bird's home in a tree many times has a round opening. If you're feeling really scientific you might ask them to speculate about why these shapes occur.

13. Treasure Hunting

It's always fun to bring home a little "treasure" to remember the hike with. A treasure is anything that is valuable to the person finding it. It could be a gold nugget, but probably it will be a pretty rock or a feather.

Activity 13.1 Find a Treasure to Take Home

Let's see what kind of treasures your kids come up with. Once they find that special object let them tell you why it is a treasure to them. Can they make up a story about that special object? That colorful rock might be a gemstone that fell from a king's crown. That feather might be from a magical bird who only drops a feather once every hundred years!

14. Nature Sings

When you are out in nature it will be a lot quieter than in the city, but if you listen, you will hear all kinds of sounds: The wind blowing through the trees, birds singing, the sound of a stream, insects buzzing around, and many more.

Activity 14.1 Hearing Nature's Sounds

Have everyone be real still and just listen for a few minutes. See how many different sounds they can detect. If someone says they can't hear a specific sound, have everyone be quiet again and listen for that sound.

Activity 14.2 Imitating Natural Sounds

Once you have heard some interesting sounds like a little waterfall or a bird singing, see who can come closest to reproducing that sound. OK, they might not end up being as pretty as birdsong, but I bet you will have a lot of fun.

Meet The Author

Hi, I'm Rick McKeon. I am currently living in beautiful Prescott, Arizona. Since retiring I have been spending time pursuing my passion for writing, playing music and teaching. I am currently producing a series of video lessons on playing the banjo and guitar, and am writing books encouraging people to appreciate nature at a deeper level.

Some of my other pursuits include hiking, backpacking, treasure hunting, exploring old ghost towns and mines, recreational mathematics, photography and experimenting with Microcontrollers.

For more about these activities check my websites at rickmckeon.com rickmckeonNature.com and rickmckeonScientific.com

Your comments are always welcome. Send me an email at rmckeon5@gmail.com

Other Books by Rick McKeon

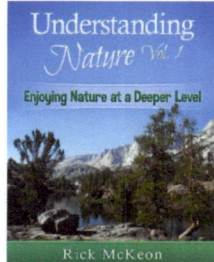 Understanding Nature Vol. 1: Enjoying Nature at a Deeper Level!
ISBN: 9781502510020

 Sierra Impressions: Images and Inspiration From the Sierras
ISBN: 9781310403699

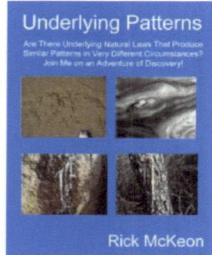 Underlying Patterns: The Search for Patterns in Nature
ISBN: 9781311783615

 You Make Us Feel Young Again!
ISBN: 9781310558108

 Amazing Fractal Images: Postcards From the Complex Plane
ISBN: 9781311990440

www.ingramcontent.com/pod-product-compliance
Lightning Source LLC
Chambersburg PA
CBHW041518280526
45792CB00004B/1297